Love Alone

CHARLES JOHNSON

authorHOUSE®

AuthorHouse™
1663 Liberty Drive
Bloomington, IN 47403
www.authorhouse.com
Phone: 1 (800) 839-8640

Published by AuthorHouse 10/15/2018

ISBN: 978-1-5462-5516-1 (sc)
ISBN: 978-1-5462-5515-4 (e)

Library of Congress Control Number: 2018909729

Print information available on the last page.

CHAPTER 1

What is love?

G od is love everything about God is love, love is the grated gift give to man, love make the world go around, it was love that God use to create the world, when everything else filets love keep going because love never fill, because God is love and God could never fall, can't you separate love from God or God from love because the two are one, when talking about God you talking love and when talking love you talking love, but when it comes He created the world

He did it out of love and that love made Him perfect. And no darkness can ever dwell in Him, because He is love, there is no separate from love, everything God did or do is love because He know no other way, before the foundation of the world God live in love and that love He created the world, have you ever wonder how God got this kind of love, He have so love that He created a world out of love and everything He did or do is perfect, in the beginning He created the world out of love and with so much love a light was born and the center of darkness the love of God is so perfect that He sent His only begotten Son Jesus Christ into the world to suffer and die for the world Sin, because His love us is perfect.

Long before the foundation of the world before anything was created God decide to created a world a perfect world and when He created this world He created it out of His perfect love therefore He being Perfect everything He did was perfect, let take a look at what God did in the beginning of the world,

Genesis 1:1-31 in the beginning God created the heavens and the earth. The earth was without form, and void and darkness was on the face of the deep.

Although God is love He is able to take that love and created the heavens and the earth and made them perfect. But the earth was void and darkness was on the face of the deep and spirit of

God His love hovering over the face of the waters. If you notch you can see the power of love working here And God said let there be light and there was light.

Let keep in mind as you read this book God is sharing with us what He did in the beginning He want us to take what He did here and use it and our everyday life, when God said let there be light and there was light, what God is telling us when darkness come into your life you have the power to called light into it, so what is light, light is only Love and where love is darkness can not stand and will not stand. We are made in the image of God and His Son see Genesis 1:26 then God said let us make man in our image according to our likeness let them have dominion over the fish of the sea over the birds of the air and over the cattle over all the earth and over every creeping thing that creeps on the earth, look how much God love us He created the earth and put every thing that man will need and He gave power over it, all this was done before any man has till the ground the love of was showed to man kind.

But let me reminder you there is also the power of darkness it to is very real if a man living in darkness he don't have the power to called anything into the light, because that man or woman is not walking in love and where there is no love there will be darkness and where darkness is no light and where there light people is blind and when people is blind the devil is there light and when the devil is your light he is seeking to killed and to destroy. But the power of love will take a person to a new high that person will be able to see things coming miles away and darkness will be able to creep up on that person, for God Himself will guided that person to the truth and darkness will flee from that person and when it returned it will still find that light still shinning, where there is love there is hope and where hope any thing is possible, because God is love see Matthew19:26 but Jesus looked at them and said to them, with men this impossible but with God all things are possible.

Where there is love there will be faith because God is love and God said without faith it is impossible to please God. And the reason God said this because He created the heavens and the earth He did it faith and anything we do differ from what God told us to is a sin and when told us you shall love the LORD your God with all your heart, with all your soul, and with all your might. Deuteronomy 6:5 in during this God will in power us to do all things in the name of Jesus, but we must love our neighbor as we love our self said the Lord Leviticus 19:18 how can we love God who we never seen and not love our neighbor whom we see every day, who is our neighbor the people we see every day that person we see in the store at the gas station in Church at work these are our neighbor

If you know your bible then you would know the story about the Good Samaritan an expert in the Law of Moses stood up and asked Jesus a question to see what he would say. Teacher he asked what must I do to have eternal life?

Jesus answered, what is written in the scriptures? How do you understand them? The man replied, The Scriptures say, love the Lord your God with all your heart, soul Strength, and mind. They also say, love your neighbors as you love yourself,

Jesus said, you have given the right answer. If you do this, you will have eternal life.

But the man wanted to show that he knew what he was talking about. So he asked Jesus, who are my neighbors?

Jesus replied:

As a man was going down from Jerusalem to Jericho, robbers attacked him and grabbed everything he had. They beat him up and ran off, leaving him half dead.

A priest happened to be going down the same road. But when he saw the man, he walked by on the other side. Later a temple helper came to the same place. But when he saw the man who had been beaten up, he also went by the other side.

A man from Samaria then came traveling along that road

when he saw the man; he felt sorry for him and went over to him. He treated his wounds with olive oil and wine and bandaged them. Then he put him on his own donkey and took him to an inn, where he took care of him. The next morning he gave the innkeeper two silver coins and said. Please take care of the man. If you spend more then this on him, I will pay you when I return, Then Jesus asked, which one of these three people was a real neighbor to the man who was beaten up by robbers? The teacher answered, the one who showed pity.

Jesus said, Go and do the same' Luke 10:25-37 after reading this story your heart should have be touch, in this age and time people all over the world need help and when we give from your heart God will make sure we never go liking for anything, just like the good Samaria man who stop and help the beat up man, the other two men who pass the beat up man they was also able to help the man, see God never put us in the path of some one who need help and we can't help them, for this is the reason why God put that person in the path that you are traveling, there is so many people in the world today who just think about there self, and many of these people are able to help other, the Lord tell us we are to bear one another's burdens, and so fulfill the law of Christ. See Gal 6:2, When God created the world He know as mankind would grow, He there would be so many people that they couldn't be counted at one point God told Abram who name became Abraham that He would blessed him with so many people that they would be like the dust of the of the earth, see Gen 13:15-16 God knew with so many people on the earth some would need help with they burdens, if God position you to help other He have supplied you with everything you need to help, so if you are able to someone help then, I remember when I was a boy my grandmother told me if I can feed myself I would have enough to feed someone else from that day until now I have not forgot what she told me, so one day I put what she told me to the test and she was right every time I cook I have always had more then enough food to go around no matter how many people needed to eat.

The key to making this way must come from the heart with faith and trust and believe, you must have faith in God.

You must believe in God.

And you must in trust God with all your heart and nothing will be impossible for you. That why is it so important for us to help people on the street just the other day I was going into the store when some one was inside the store begging people for money as they come out of the store? Why do thank people wait until we come out of the store to ask us for money? You would think they would ask you before you go in the store,

The reason why they do ask before you go in to the store, it not that they don't want to but they feel that it may hurt their chance of you given it to them, just because they are beggar don't mean they are dumb, but they think like we think, they are putting their self in our place, I would like for some one to ask me for money after I come out of the store they may have a better chance I will give it to them and they know that, this the reason why they when we come out, but there is a another reason why I think it is good for them to wait for us to come out, a reason they don't know, but could it be that God given us time to think about it before we say no, but want us to give to those who ask, for the Lord said give to him who asks you, and from him who wants to borrow from you and do not turn away. See Matthew 5:42 by giving we show love toward one another, for God love a cheerful giver, it is good to keep in mind that the person who asking for our help would be place there for your good that maybe God way giving you what you asking Him for, we give and it will be given to us, that may have prayed to God for help and we may be God way to help that person. And when I came out of the store and that person ask me for help and I don't give it to him not that I didn't have it to give I was just being mean in Spirit but God want us to have a loving Spirit, and right away my Spirit was moved as I drove off.

Life will be must more health for us if we obey the words of God.

Love make the world go round because God love for us He give us all that is needed to keep everything in it places, He give us family to love but He also give us stranger to love and when we meet people we don't know they are stranger, there love the stranger, for you were strangers in the land of Egypt. See Deut 10:18-19, let love be without hypocrisy. Abhor what is evil. Cling to what is good. Be kindly affectionate to one another with brotherly love, in honor giving preference to one another, see Romans 12:9-10. what happen to brotherly love I grow up in the south where there was nothing but brotherly love, if I have you have, if you have I have, I need you give me, you need I give you, people always when to each in the time of need and got what they needed to take care of their family.

People went out the way to help each other, but in today world love only have one meaning if you love me, then I love you what kind of love is that, the Lord ask what good is it to love some one just because they love you, what good is it, if God love us the way we love Him and give to us like we love and give to Him most of the world wouldn't make it, but God love us before the foundation of the world He didn't wait to see how much love we would returned to Him, base on the love

He show us, God is good, how many time has we heard some one say God is good, people who know God is good should never say how lucky they are because if you say God is good then their shouldn't never be a place in you heart that cause you to say am lucky. When a man use the word lucky he take away from himself and in so many words he is saying God is not in control of his life or the universe that He created, and we know that is no true, everything were created by God for God, weather then or now there is nothing new under the sun, no matter what man come up with it have already before, and the reason why this true because God created the world and everything in it the things that has past and the things to come, He know the beginning and He know the end, in the beginning God Himself walk and talked to man on earth, but after the birth of His Son Jesus Christ who was born of a woman die on the cross and rose on the third day and set at the right hand of God our heavenly father, God gave Him all power in heaven and on earth therefore everything must go before God through His Son Jesus Christ, before Jesus there is God. God is first and He will always be first, and should always be first He God almighty God the beginning and the end nothing where here before Him, and nothing will left after Him, God will live forever and forever there will no end to God. But there is some who don't believe that, so how do we this because God is love and love never die, but will live forever, when everything failed love is the way, people really don't know the they have if they live in love, everything they want in life money, cars home whatever they can have the only thing God ask us to do is love one another, just love is all it take it the differ between have what you want and keep it. Or working yourself to death and never having time to enjoy what you working so hard to get, and leaving it behind for some one else to enjoy it, Love is the key to having a good life.

In the book of Deuteronomy 30:19 I call heaven and earth as witnesses today against you, that I have set before you life and death, blessing and cursing: therefore choose life, that both you and your descendants may live:

God told us to choose life and live all we need to do is love another, put God first therefore we will walk in the light with Him. He will give you understanding in all things and nothing will be impossible for you, never will be able to creep up on you, nothing will catch you by surprise, you will be able see things coming your way good or bad.

When we walk in the light with God darkness have no places in our life because light is love and love rules over darkness, and when do come and it will come but your light will shine even more, because God Himself has said He would never leave you alone, and no darkness will never be able to stand before God. When we walk in love we will understand the things of God. He will not let you walk in darkness, He will bless you, you will have whatever your heart desire and more can a man need or want to have his heart desire, so no matter where you go make friends and always be ready to help some one and help as many as God supple there need in your hand, and what ever it may be give thanks to God and trust Him to meet the need He will He will never let us down, why because we are trusting in Him and believing in what He said in His words. Remember God is good, when we get up in the morning we should give God thanks

Psalm 8:4-8 what is man that you mindful of him,

And the son of man that you visit him, for you made him a little lower than the angels and you crowned him with glory and honor. You have made him to have dominion over the works of your hands:

You have put all things under his feet,

This is how much God love mankind that He put man over all the works of His hand under His feet that is a lot of love. If you love your neighbor as God command us to do don't worry about how your neighbor treat you. God will take care of and your neighbor. God is a good God He will not let anyone mistreat you in get away with it. On the other hand if we do what we do out of love what dose it matter what our neighbor do, you can bet the love you show them will stay with them and whatever they do to you and other in the wrong way will burned in their heart, if someone do right by you or I and we do wrong by them right away we feel guilt. And right away we look a way to make it up to them, and something we get the chance to make up to that person and sometime we don't the feeling we get when we do wrong is order by God Himself, all sin and all wrong will be paid for and no one is above that. Life is to short for anything that is bad we here today and gone tomorrow we may rise with the morning sun but who to know if we will set with the going down of the sun, so be happy everyday live life with love it not how someone love you, but it how much you love you give out. If no one love you but God that should be more the enough and you know that love will be real.

Grace, mercy, and peace from God the Father and Christ Jesus our Lord.

CHAPTER 2

What happen when there is no love?

N ow that I have the first chapter of this competed I feel like I am able to do the second chapter with faith, not that I did the faith in the first chapter I did with out some kind of faith, it would hard for anyone to write a book.

In the first chapter I talk about love, the second chapter is very much about love from the dark side, the first chapter was about love and light the second chapter is about darkness and no love. It is true love absent from light is darkness so many people has die and gone to hell, because they refuse to let love in their heart. The heart can only put what we store inside, and so many people have missed the mark in fell into the outer darkness and hell becomes their home forever. And nothing God can do because in the beginning God gave everything it limited, even darkness has it limited and God will take and chance it because He is God and from the beginning He set His rules. And given all it limited, like the sea, the ocean the wind all have there limited. And we get off the past that God has given us to follow we then step into another zone and who know what in that zone God know what in that zone that why He warned us not to talk in darkness.

Psalm 107:10 those who sat in darkness and in the shadow of death, bound in affliction and irons. When people live in darkness there is a lot of consequences,

Sin bring about consequences all sin come with a price to pay, if you know you are living in sin you must know there is a price to pay, if you are in a relationship and not marriage and have sex.

And at the same time the verse I read in the bible stay with me. Proverbs 5:15 drink water from your own cistern, and running water from my own well. There is also another verse that read don't cover your neighbor goods, the sad thing about these verses for me I understood them, I knew the meaning of them, but I choose to keep going in my sin.

Somewhere down the line I knew I would pay for my sin because I knew all sin must be paid for and no one get out of that for God is not a favor person. He love us that why He tell us not to do it because He what will happen, Sin separate us from God no matter who we think we are sin will keep you in the dark, and if we living in darkness Satan is your father, like it or not it the truth, and nothing God can do to help us until we turned away from our Sin and repent ask God to forgive you and never look back and never do that sin again. He will forgive you, but you need to understand how God forgiven work, no one can go around living in sin and ask God to forgive them and keep doing the same sin and ask God to forgive you, let me tell you, you are wasting your time, you must stop during what you are doing and it must come from the heart, for God know the heart of man, because He search all man heart, because we do come from the heart,

Take a few second and think about what you are doing, weather is good or bad and if you search deep enough you will find what you do come from your heart, that how God made us, it is His way to knew if we are being truthful or not, it the easy God way to know us. See 1 Samuel 16:7 But the LORD said to Samuel, do not look at his appearance or at the height of his stature, because I have refused him, for the LORD does not see as man see; for man looks at the outward appearance, but the LORD looks at the heart, we can't fool God He created us, so when we go to God for anything it must be from the heart, and if it from your heart God will hear you. He will answerer us, it all up to you how quit and how bad you want God help, all the lone when I was dealing with this marriage woman I ask to help to get out of the sin I was now living in, He knew my heart and things begin to happen in the right way, but the price to pay for what I had do was far from over, I saw some light, but the end was out of reach

Be care what you ask for you just may get it and more. We have been through a lot in the five years we been together and not all have been good mostly bad, people get marriage everyday for the wrong reason most of the time the woman are looking for a man who is stable and who can meet her needs, but always picking the wrong one, she is easy deceived by the things she see, they are pleasant to her eyes. Therefore when her eyes become open from that dark world she been living in most of time she feel that it is to late, in most cases it is to late. But she should never give up life out side of marriage is not all dead, but whatever she do she must never fall back into the way of the world, I have heard so many who was marriage and now divorce, or getting a divorce say they will never get marriage again, and now have open themselves up for all kind of things to come and mostly bad things, surly there will time when things seem to be going good but she must be very careful that the devil is not setting her up for the kill, because if we walking in the dark one must remember he or she are not walking alone, we never walk alone if we walk in the light we are in God hand.

If we walk in the dark we are the devil hand there is no middle man, so the woman who is always the easy one to be deceived because he walk my sight it is pleasant to her eyes so will be most likely of the two to go though life being bitter in any relationship because the man know what she are looking for, therefore he know what to do to get the woman. If he want decide to keep her he will make her his wife, if he decide she any the one for him he will cheat on her, so the woman need to be very careful about the life she choose. It is sad to say she is the one always being use, because the love she seek and the road she take to find it lead her in many dark places, but if she slow down and think about the power she really have when it come to a man she will never have a problem she can't deal with, for God is no favorable person but He created the world and He made all the rules and the person make the rules have to power, And

God have the power, and he gave some to man some to woman but the power to over see the earth he gave man.

The woman in today world are complaining about how fear they not being treaded compare to man but on the other hand in the relationship they look for the man to love them and tread them right, which is their right, but on the other hand they want the power God has given man to over see them, now man have begin to take the back seat to woman leave the world wide open for Satan to do his thing, but you can believe this when the is not the head all hell break lose and a male is still in charge, and for all the woman who think they have power over man and this is a woman world now, you should keep in mind Satan the devil is a he and he king of deceived, you disobey God in the garden He is a male but you listing to the devil who is also a he, for God is love and He gave you the way and you choose not to listing to Him. He gave you man and you still don't want to listing, but the devil you obey, and never here a person say they power over the devil, why is that because they the devil is real and they want to say anything to get on the devil bad side but weather they know it or the devil doses have a good side he is all darkness all the time he come to kill steal and destroy and he is good what he dose he don't turn to the right or the left he is what he is a destroyer, he play for keep.

CHAPTER 3

What happen to the woman when she walks alone?

W hat to a woman when she choose to walks a lone away from God our Father and Lord Jesus Christ and earthly man, she will never walk alone although she choose to away from God, Lord Jesus, and man the devil waited in the wind with open arms to welcome her, to his world the world of darkness and he don't make her any deal in the book of Matthew 4; 1-11 then Jesus was led up by the Spirit into the wilderness to be tempted by the devil,(when the woman choose to walk on her on there is no reason for the devil to really temp her, she have already open herself up for him to come in) and when He had fasted forty days and forty nights afterward He was hungry.(when to woman choose to walk alone she to will get hungry and the devil will be waiting to offer what she will believe to be good) but first he must take his turn waiting for to turned away from God Lord Jesus and man, because the power has been given out from God the created to the Son His only Son who gave some to man, when the woman take the role to be her own boss away from God, Lord Jesus and man who God have given the power to have dominion over all the things He created on the earth. So the devil choose the man to do his dusty work, why because he knew the woman herself can be a great deceiver herself she have the power to get man to do whatever she want good or bad she had can get him to do it. Just like God who don't saw favor, the devil have his way to get things done and because he is a male he take the easy way out and go to the woman, just like in church the man have a hard time doing what another telling what to do, the bottle line is a male have a hard time submit to another male. But most female don't have trouble with it as long as the other female don't cross her, but if she do all hell break lose. And that what the devil all about destroy any good in any and all things he is the devil, if you take the time to look around in today world you don't need to look far to see how far the female have come, they hold a number of powerful position, and most of them mean good but with some much going on in their life it is easy for the devil to deceive them, the man of the home is not longer the head of the family, the kids are running wild because now the man and woman are now in competition with each other, so what do we have the man who God place to be head of the family and to over see them, have now lost some ground to look to God for help, if he has lost his position in the home how can God help if his wife is out of order and sooner or later if any children in the home respect for the mother or father will disappear now the devil will have his way, all peace will leave the home so now the home become a house. That run like a hotel everyone come and leave as they please, because a man will not stand back and let the woman run the home no matter how must money she make, her money will never over take his position in the home, what could happen he may play the role to let her believe she is in change, you bet he is look ease were to lay his head and be head of the home, there is only home and head like it on not that the way it is two king can't rule under the same roof, they why they been given the position of king the head.

When she walk alone she become lonely sad, and depression most of us live in what appears to be a loneliness- producing society where rapid change, people avoid each other in every change that get, in the attempt to find closeness. People need help develop intimate relationship

p with God. Many people spend a lot of their money on seeking counseling, and if the counselor is not a child of God that is money going to waste, but a woman who walk alone, she walk in darkness.

CHAPTER 4

She never looks back

Domestic violence has a serve physical, emotional and financial impact on its victims. The physical injuries can be severe and they usually get worse over a period of time. Many domestic violence episodes end in homicide.

A unique feature of domestic violence is that the victimization comes from one whom the victim trusts. Causing more pain than the physical injuries the victim suffers is the sense of betrayal.

A spouse's sense of control and trust has been violated and the victim is left feeling extremely vulnerable. The violence often affects the attitudes of victims and makes it difficult for them to develop healthy interpersonal relationships with others. Many victims are financially dependent on their spouse, and if they leave their spouse, often with children, they are often without any financial support.

No one, regardless of one's circumstances, has the right to use physical violence to control, intimidate or punish another human being. Put yourself in the place of the victim of domestic violence and imagine how you would feel if you been physically harmed by your spouse.

With split lips, burns and scalds, torn scalps, broken teeth, and bruised necks, she headed to Las Vegas with a smile on her face, and laughing to herself, she had just walked away from a relationship for more than twenty years, and most of those years had been in some farm of domestic abuses, many day she thought of killing herself but with a child she knew she needed to be there for her child. It was about 11; pm when he walked in the door his clothes was blooded his face were bruised put some how he was able to drive his self home. After leaving work he made a stop to the bar to have a few drink before going home, and beating her they been together for more then twenty years but never got marriage, she didn't work but they had three kids together and she financially dependent on him. So if she leaves she wouldn't have any where to go. But on this night things was about to change, she had made plan to take her kids and leave, but the time wasn't right not that, but when he came to the door she was standing there, but he walk right past her and never said a work to her, it was the first time he came home and never said something to her, but he went to the bed room and laid down and when to sleep when she saw him do that she knew something was wrong with him, but she never said a word to him.

CHAPTER 5

Stop speaking things into existed

Most people in relationship weather marriage or singer doesn't realize the things they say to each other, can cause trouble in the relationship, the words they speak is very much a live, when people say things to each other weather they know or not they are calling them things into existed, everyone need to know every word we speak we put something into action good or bad, nothing we say just go away, the creator of this world that is God will judge us on every word we speak, we can do a lot of good with the word we speak and we can also destroy a man with word, let keep in mind that God speak is were good, He spoke things into existed He also spoke and thing were destroyed

In the book of Genesis the first chapter it tells us what God did with the dark space. In the beginning God created the heavens and the earth. The earth was without form, and void and darkness was on the face of the deep. And the Spirit of God hovering over the face of the waters, then God said let there be light and there was light.

Here we see what happen when God spoke words because the power is in the word that we speak, you may say this what God did but you/ we are created in the image of God.

Genesis 1;26 then God said let us make man in Our image, according to Our likeness; let them have dominion over the fish of the sea, over the birds of the air, and over all the cattle over all the earth. In His image He credit male and female. God have giving power to called things into existed, and weather you know it or not God love so much that He gave us the same power He use to created the world He gave to us, but for us It came with a price and the is what you do it will returned to you in the same way, if you forgive He will forgive us, so don't wasted you time asking God to forgive you of your sins if having forgiven your brother, God don't work that way, whatever you do to other will come back to you, people spend all their time doing wrong toward others, and run to God forgiven. But they themselves has not gone to the other person asking for forgiven, God said his words will not returned to Him void, God said the world the will pass way but by no mean will His words pass, so if we do good then good will follow, if we do bad, then bad will follow, not one who do bad will receive good, but anyone who do good from their heart will be blessed, do you know that the words you speak cannot escape from the universe but travel through space and come by to you every word we speak,

It would good to know how the invisible things in the universe are God way to show His power that He has place in us when we believe in Him. When we believe in Him we will obey His word and when we obey His words we are able to do what He did in the beginning of His creation and that was called things that was invisible to become visible,

CHAPTER 6

When to give up sex

W hen is the right time for a woman to hand over the key to her life, the key that open the door to her heart, the most important? Thing so have to give a man, she spend her whole life waiting for the right man to come alone, to give herself to, it is so important to that if she rape everything she has shut down, in most case she never the same again, she try hard to over come what happen to her, but only time will tell, something that so important to her when is the right time to give it up, sex is what am talking about, how long can she keep herself pure, I believe most women want to get marriage first before having sex but in most case that never happen, no matter what so do to keep herself pure there will always be a man looking to sweet talk her in having sex, so when is the right time for the woman to have sex, when she is marriage, because if she marriage her power is not lost, because he given to her husband and that could be a good thing, but if having sex outside of marriage she give up her power that God given her to give to her husband, you may ask what power, the power to get the man to do anything she want him to do, twenty-four hours day she have the power to make him do what she want. And he will he will anything to get her in bed, and the one who hold the power is the one calling the shot, a woman who have someone in her life a boyfriend or a man friend and she have not had sex with him, she make the rules, and there is nothing the man can do. If many women use this power the man will be begging them to get marriage, or they will move on, but you can bet if he leave without having sex with you he keep coming around until you get marriage to someone ease, or to him, if he want to be with you he will marriage you, other hand how long will stay it really don't matter because you did what you needed to do and that was get marriage before sex, and you still have the power to how long your husband will stay around, things may change a little but you still have the power to keep him around if you want him around, and he being your husband you should want him around, one thing you may want to do is stay away from wanting to know about his pass relationship, it is an old say what you don't know want hurt you, so why look into the pass of someone, what good will it do, if you or partner feel that you need to let the other one know something about your pass you will tell them,

Every woman knows what a man from her. Sex they why she have the power over the man before she sleep with him, because the moment she sleep with and don't have herself together, will be the will be the moment she give her power away, and when she lose her power, she will very littler time to get back, because one or two thing will happen, (1) the man will immediately feel that he has you right where he want you, he will continue to play the good guy if he want to see you again, although he may feel that you are his girl or woman, but having sex with him the first time, he don't feel that have the power, not yet, so he keep on saying and doing the things you like, to get you in bed the second time,

He want any more time trying to get you in bed the second and third time because the he can get you in bed the more you will give him your only strong power, because he know you may not like the way he have sex, and all men know if a woman don't like the way a men have sex it could be the first and the last time she will sleep with him, so between the first time and the third time he will fool himself to believe he got a chance, he will only hope so,

Warranting

Now that you have sleep with this man outside of marriage what should do now, remember there will be consequences to pay for you sin, sleeping someone other then your husband is a sin before God.

What do you do now, ask God to forgive you and stop having sex with this man until you get marriage, just because sleep with him, don't mean you getter keep on doing it, now is the best time to talk to him about marriage, if he say ok and ask you to marriage him, then you did good, if he tell you he love you and you love him then getting should at the top your list, never waste time waiting around to get marriage, because sin knocking at your door and you don't want to die in sin, because if you do hell wait for you, so you have lot to think about, is this good enough for you to marriage, will he be a good husband, a good father, is he a man of God. Just because he sleep with you don't mean he don't love or he not a child of God but what it do mean he is out the well of God. And it never good to marriage anyone out the well of God, People do get marriage all the time out of the well of God and the marriage never last, if God not in it, it will never last, only what God dose will last, and whatever you do please don't marriage this man for what he have or what he can do for you, because gave marriage to do the right things, when people get marriage they support to do the right things, but when you marriage someone for the wrong reason you have already brought trouble to yourself and your marriage, only you know if this man is the one for you, beside God know your heart, this man could be a good man but he my not be for you, or you for him, but keep it real, because some where down the road if you marriage him for the wrong reason your life will catch hell because one thing you can bet on your marriage will be tested, and the devil will come with everything he had to end it.

So many woman make the mistake of getting marriage to some one they know they shouldn't marriage but fool themselves to believe when they get marriage she will change him, woman all over the world have wasted most of their live trying change a man and it never happen, and when she do everything she can to change him but never find a way then she mad at the world, when the only people she should be mad with is herself, and now she let devil have let the devil into her marriage and all hell break a loose, but weather she know it or not the devil enter the marriage the very moment she told herself I can change him, it was the devil taking to her then, only God can change a person, and he will not change anyone unless that person ask Him, if a man don't want to change nothing can change him, but something could happen in his life that may or could being about a change, and there will be many things he will face if he walking in sin, that could cause him to have a change of heart,

So make sure this is the man for you, and you are the woman for him, he just my be the man for you, but on the other hand you may not be the woman for him, and whatever you do don't fool yourself believing he love you. Make sure he loves you. There are many way you can tell if a man love you, I will you some of them later in the book, the first thing you need to do is to get to know him, his way what he like what he don't like take the time to look him up and down, the things you like don't worry about it, if not broken why fit it, but the things you don't like keep a close look at them, because there will be things about him that you ant going to like, just like you there will be things about you he not going to like, he is a man and you are a woman, you are differ in many ways the things you don't like talk to him about it, I mean set him down in a nice way and talk to him not at him but to him, and when you are talking to him keep in mind he is a man and you are marriage to him he is not only a man he is your husband, and if he not your husband take a close look at the consequences for your sin in sleep with someone you not marriage too, and when you set him down talk about whatever he is doing that you don't like, and see how he handle it, it is very important that you listing to the first thing that come out of his mount, and wait for him to finish talking before you say what you want to say never cut him off, just set and listing, to what he has to say there may be a time when he is talking that you may want to cut him off and say something but don't, because the time you feel you need to say something is the time he may give you what you been waiting to hear weather it good or bad, some women think men are fool, and that a man don't think it not that he don't think about what he going to do but in most cases he don't really care, or he do what he want and face the consequences, but most of the time he not ready for what the consequences going to bring, so make life easy for yourself and take the short cut, what I mean about the short cut, use the power God gave you and use it well, it is the way to happiness, but you much practice what you preach, and sometime human for to do that, and what happen when we don't practice what preach it always catch up to us and catch us off guard and we find ourselves wounded and asking yourself what do I do now, in the next chapter I will talking about play games in the relationship.

CHAPTER 7

Playing game in the relationship

Only one person is good when it come to playing game in a relationship and that is the woman, a man don't know how to play game in the relationship he will failed 100 percent of the time when he try to go head to head with the woman he is no match for the woman, she will win all the time. But let me play it safe by saying 95 percent of the time she will win. And the reason why I said 95 percent of the time, be we do have the young girl who just starting out who just maybe get crotch up dealing with an older man who will take her to school in the relationship but you can be it wont take her long catch on to what he is doing, but over all the had no game when it come to the woman, but on the other hand when it come to him playing a game with another man when things will be differ. Because in that game men play to win, the game of sports is what I am talking about just like the woman who plays the game of sports she know she will never be able to beat the man in his own game, any woman who thinks differ is fooling herself, just like the man who things he can out play the woman in the relationship he is fooling himself,

A man only has one goal and that is to get the woman in bed that is why he is able to go out, and cheat, he don't think with his brains. He offer use his littler head to think for him, he has no real plans when he meet the woman his only plans is to get her in bed, and she know that, and when you know what the other person plans are you can use it to get what you want because you know what he want. The power be lone to the woman, the game is hers to play and if she choose to play the game she hold all the card. She is the coach, she the quarterback, she called all the plays, and the man will do whatever she called, but like all good coaches they have away of calling bad plays that can cause them to lose the game.

Most women play the game to win in the relationship but what she forget is that she taking the chance of losing at the end, because the game that they play. Are game men will catch on to, because if the man is smart he will find away to ask another female, and just like another man knows another, a woman knows another woman, playing games in the relationship is never a good ideal, because you don't what the other person thinking in believe me it may no be good, if your husband or man friend call you on the cell and don't answers his called because you are mad but he know that you are mad he just may give you a break, but if this keep going on because you decide to make him sweat and make thinks you may be doing something when you not doing nothing what a chance you are taking. It just a game you playing with your mate, a woman is so good playing the game she just take the short cut, and the man never know the differ, that just how far she is out in front of the man, so know the way to the man mind, and spend very littler time trying to reach his heart.

And when a woman get to know a man her man that man is in trouble, the woman spend a lot of time trying see what make a man tick, and when she find out make him tick she waste no time push his button, when she think about playing game with his feeling it offering back fried on her and she find herself in an abused relationship, that could lead to her death, the bad think about playing with a man feeling she set herself up for a world of trouble, the more she play with the man feeling the more the man fall for her, and will do anything gain her love, he become blind to her game, and if she play her game right and keep it smooth she will gained his heart, and if she don't want his heart while playing with his feeling she need to know what go around come around, but he who catch to second always get the worse of the deal, because play back is a bitch, and what a feeling to deal with, it like being cut on when someone is cutting on you and you which you was dead, but death is slow to come,

It is never a good idea to play with some one feeling, so be real then if the other person get hurt it is likely you will keep yourself clear from getting hurt, because you let it be know how you feel, the other person may not like it so you kept real, you never want to hurt anyone weather you mean to or not when you hurt someone you will face the consequences and who know what the pay will be, for years people be mistreating each other and believing some how they will get away with it, but come to find out the table has turned, so now what you going to do, it is never a good ideal for a woman to get catch up in her own game, a woman should never play her with a man, she don't need too,

If the man like her he will let her know by his action, after all she have what it take to win him over, and if not then he may not be the one for her, we all have a soul mate and no one said it would be easy finding them, when you find your soul mate or he find you, you both will know it, most people miss out on their soul mate for many reason, but the most coming one, they is in a relationship with someone ease who just maybe the wrong one. And when Mr. comes alone she miss out on him, and when that happen the other man will pay for her unhappy, to many people get free from someone they have try for years to out and they do get out but the game they played with someone want let them be free because it time to pay the consequences for the sin they have done, and most of the time the man is not willing to wait around and wait on her to get herself together regarding another man. But men are difference women when it come to that, a woman will wait on a man to leave a woman, but the man will only wait on a woman to leave a men if she really going to leave, he will only give her a littler time to make up her mind to leave, on the other hand if he don't care about her he will give her all the time she want but you can bet he will have someone on the side.

A good relationship is a marriage one people not to quit to run out on each other, because they know they are marriage and no matter what happen they will deal better with it, but when two people are going together and when things get bad they can go there own way with nothing to lose, but when two become one they have a lot to lose.

CHAPTER 8

How to find a good man

You don't let him find you, a woman should always keep in mind the man is the hunter, he has always been the hunter, man is know to be called a dog by woman this not why he was giving the name the hunter by natural he the male that what make him the hunter, and when the hunter go to hunt he has in mind what he is going to hunt, in most case when he is hunting he always come up on something he really not looking for, but spend some time seeing what it is all about before move on.

There is only one man the male with differing quartz of men, the good, the bad, the ugly, and when I say ugly I mean ugly, when speak of ugly am not talking about outer man the way the man look am talking about the inter man, the man always has a way to deceived the woman this is the man only game, and believe it or not he is good at it, most women make the mistake to believed most men don't have this game, but what she don't know the man is picking her a part piece by piece to see if she the one for him, it may take some time for him to completed this test, and 90 percent of the time the woman want know she is been graded on everything she do. Because if the man really like her he may prolong the test, just to make sure she the one, most men don't go around just marriage a woman just to marriage her she will met him needs before he ask her to marriage him.

So if the woman looking for Mr. right and she is the one seeking him she have already place herself in the dark and we know what the darkness hold, nothing good come from walking in the darkness.

Whenever a woman find a man she put herself in a bad position from the begin of the relationship, and here is why the man think if she is bold enough to go out and look for a man she would bold to go out and look again when the storm come in the relationship because the storm will come and when it do the man want to make sure he has a strong woman in his corner, most all men feel the same about a female who go out to find a man and go up to him and ask him to be her man, most women don't do it this way and not this open about it but it is just what they do, the woman should always keep herself in the position to be hunted by the man, that way she have the power in the relationship because the man came to her, people who been together for a long time

CHAPTER 9

I cross the line

O God please forgive me I cross the this time, the consequences I have paid for crossing this line has been more then enough, but if more then enough would end now I would feel some release, but I don't see any release in sight.

Always remember the more the woman want to leave her husband and home, the more she want to be with someone ease, if she ready to leave to home she may not even be in love with the other man but for now it a way out and not be alone she will take that chance, sometime it work other it don't but here is the consequence for that, she through about her plans and how she would work it, some time it work other time it don't, if she just want to use the man to get way because he is nice to her she most likely to take that road, and if the man feeling her and that way because he have a woman, and it is a budded called, it all good but the only thing about that the longer this go on one of going to start having feeling real feeling for the other person that will change the whole plans, there is never a way out with out someone getting feeling hurt and that my friend is just the beginning of the consequences.

There is two kind of relationship that is a long shot to make, but it could happen, but it going to take real love from the two of them, you can rest for shore there will be consequences to pay, and if the two of you work together thought them it can work,

A relationship where other people involved

Marriage people who break their promise to one another and go their own way leaving the one behind hurt, people work hard to get together when other people involved, always keep in mind marriage people is danger people and the reason be God the Father who created the heaven and the earth is on their side, whatever you do stay away from marriage people, not matter what the woman tell you how bad things is at home just wait for them to go their way, and even then if she live in the house that her and her x husband and she live in together when they were together, it would be a very good ideal not to go that home for awhile, and never spend the night there until it all done and finish between them, here what you do put yourself in the other man shoes, then you will know how you would feel that man just may feel the same way you do, it a bad feeling truth me I know I been there, even now as I write this book I am still having a hard time dealing what I did, how I would take it but a man got to do what a man got to do, from the first time I begin to write this book some things has change and some are still the same, but for the most things have gotten better, Charlize has improve a lot she is so bright, she is pass smart, at the age of four she can do almost everything on her own and do it right, she is so bright that she know anything she ask you and it is not the truth she will tell you that ant right and she will get mad at you, I never see a child so smart while so young, she is truly from God.

The world is filled with children everywhere and charlize is a child from God I really believe that not because am her father because it true we are God creation but some of us believe and many don't, God gave all of us a mind to choose but and the end He will have the last say, God created us all and give us everything we needed to live in this world everything and nothing was unlit but man thought he needed more, in today world money is everything and seem like everyone is willing to do anything to get it.

You got money you can do just about anything and get away with it, but if you a child of God the world don't have enough stuff to buy with all the money God have for him who love Him, it was God who said God so loved the world He gave His only son, and we know this to be true because we are still here, and we still here because His Son died and rose on the third day just as He said He would, no matter what people say because of Him the world move on but one day it to will end, then God will be seen by all and judged us all no one will and I mean no one will escape that day, young, old, good, bad, will stand before God to see where he or she will send the rest of their life whether it be with Him in heaven or hell the lake of fire from Him man have the chance to pick one of the two. But he only have to one because the one he don't pick that one don't matter. If pick the one to be with God he will live forever and light on he will have no more problem and all his trouble is over. Have you through about being with your created the one that created the whole world. you will see Him as He is. What a good feeling that would be how happy you will be. But what will happen if you miss the boat. How bad that would be. Thank about it setting around all day long in hell with the devil. Peace or hell. Happy or sad I have a few dreams I would like to share with you,

And I believe these Dreams trying to tell me something about my relationship with God.

CHAPTER 10

Standing Alone

W hat happen when a man standalone he too walk in darkness.

When a man stand-alone he put himself in and the dark he who is in the dark he can see nothing of God plans for man. Because this man is blind and when I speak ok man iam talking man and woman man believe if he being alone he will not have trouble. to that man life is bitter sweet this is what man think when he put his life in his own hand. GOD had a son and His son need Him so why man think he don't need God, Genesis 2;18 and God said it is not good that man should be alone. The Lord knows best for mankind. And it was God who created man and it was God who said he would never leave man Hebrews 13'5 let your conduct be without covetousness. And be with such things as you have. For He Himself has said I will never leave you or forsake you. When a man standalone he is bold being bold is a very powerful thing but you bet that God is with man and when I say man am talking about man and woman. The man any man who have faith in God. That man walk in the light. It was God who created the world for He gave and He give life today God is good and He is good all the time and if you don't believe me try Him for yourself. And see what happen. I live the American dream I have a beautiful home five cars and suv I have BMW-a jeep wrangler-Tahoe-a ford flex-ford mustang and very good income. And if I want more I can have more. I beg you to try God for yourself. No one told me this I am telling you because this happen to me my life have been good GOD did it for me and He able to it for you. And all you need to do it truth Him. Believe in Him most all have faith in Him. I did things my way it got me nowhere but headache what a bad place to be without God. And you have the devil standing with you. You are still alone. Because the devil is good for nothing but to killed and to destroy a man life. Anything God is for the devil don't anything to do with it. I got baptize when I was very young I believe in God then and I believe in God now. Just to let you know I believe God is with me. I will share a few Dreams I have had and I took them as God trying to tell me something.

DREAM #1

When I was a very young boy I was living with my grandmother. We all called her big mommy she raise us me and my two brother and one sister there was a night club down the street from the house. And there was a grocery store that was not too far from the night club. Every now and then big mommy would send me to the grocery store to pick some grocery. And I had to past the night club to get to grocery store. So one evening I was on my way back home when I saw this man coming out of the club he was drake. So I stood there in the park lot to see what this was drake man was. Going to do when he got to his car he pulls his keys out of his pocket and he did that I saw money came out with the keys. And that gave me an ideal. I told myself that I should get up in the morning and come up her to club and look for money. So one night i dream I woke up on Sunday morning and I went up to the club to look for money and while I was looking someone called my name and I look around to see who was there I saw no one so I went back to look from money and a second time someone called my name. I look for someone I saw no one. So again I went back to looking for money. And again I went back to look for money. So for the third time someone called my name. so I stop and I look around the whole parking lot I saw no one and when I went to look for money again something told me to look up. So I look up and in the blue sky I saw the face of JESUS He was looking down on me. I stood there for about 10 to 15 second looking up and just like that the face I saw vanishes away into the blue clear sky. I don't know what the Dream mean. But I do know it mean something.

DREAM#2

I Dream I was standing outside on a rainy day the sky was cover with big black rolling clouds the rain was pouring down and while I was stand there I remember seeing another man standing beside me I did not know the man as I stood there in the rain I remember the rain stop and the clouds open up and I saw a new city the was made of what look like gold and it had lights all around it. I did not see inside of the city I only saw on the outside of it. I remember turning to the man next to me. And point to what I saw and I ask him could see that and I remember him telling me no.

DREAM # 3

I Dream I was standing in the bottle of a canyon and it was raining I was looking up to find a way out but it was no way out for me the rain kept pouring down and filling the canyon the rain was filling the canyon with water at no time I was in danger for my life I remember the canyon was being fill with water. But some way I stated on top of the water and I made it to the top. And when I got to the top the rain stop and the sun came out and all I could see was beautiful flowers everywhere I look. They was all around me.

DREAM #4

I was standing in the midst of a burning build I was in the midst of fire and the fire was all around me. And I had no way out I remember I was not hurt. I remember the fire stop and what look like a hand reach in the fire and pull me out it pick me up and it took me straight up to the sky and when I got so far up from the earth I saw what look like a shadow of a hand waving over the earth and the fire started to burning I was taking out unharmed and I was not hurt.

I have many more Dreams I can share with. But not right now I do believe the LORD trying to tell me something.

Printed in the United States
By Bookmasters